WHALES

THE WILDLIFE IN DANGER SERIES

Louise Martin

Rourke Enterprises, Inc.
Vero Beach, Florida 32964

LIBRARY OF CONGRESS
Library of Congress Cataloging-in-Publication Data

Martin, Louise, 1955-
  Whales / by Louise Martin.

    p. cm. — (Wildlife in danger)
    Includes index.
    Summary: Describes the twelve species of whales,
threats to their existence, and efforts of the World Wildlife
Fund to save whales from extinction.
    ISBN 0-86592-988-2
    1. Whales — Juvenile literature.   2. Endangered species
— Juvenile literature.   3.Wildlife conservation — Juvenile
literature.   [1. Whales. 2 Rare animals. 3. Wildlife
conservation.]   I. Title.   II. Series:
Martin, Louise, 1955-
Wildlife in danger.
QL737.C4M313   1988
333.95'9 - dc19   88-10313
                                   CIP
                                   AC

*Title page photo: Southern Right
Whale (Eubalaena australis)*

TABLE OF CONTENTS

WHALES

Humans have hunted whales for centuries. In the Arctic regions, whales provided Eskimos with many of their everyday needs. Eskimos ate whale flesh, which is rich in vitamins, and used whale bones to make tools. The whales' thick layer of fat, called **blubber**, was melted down to make lamp oil. The whales' sharp teeth were used for cutting and for making fish hooks.

Eskimos still hunt whales

EARLY WHALING

In those early days, whales were hunted from a canoe, using hand-held harpoons. Sometimes the tips of the harpoons were poisoned so that the hunters did not have to wrestle with the whale. They left it floating in the sea until it was dead. Then they towed it to shore. This hunting did not kill whales in great numbers. It was not until Europeans arrived in North America that the real damage was done.

A modern harpoon is fired at a fin whale

THE GROWTH OF THE WHALING INDUSTRY

Whales were already scarce in the eastern part of the Atlantic Ocean, near Europe. They had been hunted there for years. When people began to sail across the Atlantic to North America, they found whales in abundance. The Europeans used whales for different purposes than the Eskimos. They, too, melted down the blubber to make oil, but they used the whale bone to make fashionable corsets for ladies. They did not eat the whale meat, but just wasted it.

A large whale is cut up at a whaling station

THE INTERNATIONAL WHALING COMMISSION

The demand for whales was high in all parts of the world. They were hunted in every ocean, and soon there were few left anywhere. Twelve species were hunted more than any other, and in 1946, the **International Whaling Commission** was formed to protect these twelve species from becoming **extinct**. The commission decides which kind of whale, and how many, **whalers** are allowed to catch. That way they can be sure that there will always be plenty of whales left in the world's oceans.

Hunting whales is a bloody business

The graceful tail flukes of a blue whale

Gray whales migrate south along the west coast of the United States

BLUE WHALES

Of twelve protected species of whales, the three most at risk are the blue whale, the gray whale, and the right whale. Blue whales are the largest marine mammals in the world. They can grow up to 100 feet long. Because blue whales are so big, their blubber yields a lot of oil. This made them the whalers' favorite catch. Of the original 220,000 blue whales found in the northern **hemisphere**, only 1,100 are now left.

Two gray whales swim at the surface

GRAY WHALES

Gray whales live in the northern part of the Pacific Ocean during the summer. In the winter they **migrate** along the coast of the western United States to southern California and Mexico, where their babies are born. The females find a sheltered **lagoon** where they can look after the **calves** for the first few months after they are born. Years ago, whalers used to come to these lagoons to hunt the gray whales. They were easy to catch and they killed them by the hundreds. By the end of the nineteenth century, almost a hundred years ago, there were very few gray whales left.

A southern right whale breaches

NORTHERN RIGHT WHALES

There are two kinds of right whales. Northern right whales live in the northern hemisphere, and southern ones live in the southern hemisphere. Northern right whales are the rarest whales in the world. Scientists think there are only about 300 left. Studies have shown that the population of northern right whales may be increasing by only three percent each year. This is more slowly than southern right whales, who are increasing by about seven percent a year.

right whale shows its baleen plates

SOUTHERN RIGHT WHALES

Some southern right whales migrate to Argentina each year. The **World Wildlife Fund**, an organization that saves rare animals and birds from extinction, has been studying the whales there. Scientists are trying to find out whether the whales will be hurt by Argentina's developing industry. Right now, there are only about 3,000 southern right whales, compared to an original estimate of 100,000.

A group of seabirds feed on a dead whale

HOW WE CAN HELP

Organizations like the World Wildlife Fund and the International Whaling Commission are working to help the whales. The whaling industry is much more controlled than it used to be, but other threats to the whales still exist. Our modern living pollutes their home, the oceans, with poisonous waste. These wastes kill their food as well as damaging their water. In addition, our high-powered ships disturb the whales and interfere with their communication signals. It is sad to think that our way of life may eventually mean the end of life for whales.

Glossary

blubber (BLUH ber) - a thick layer of fat under the skin of a
  sea mammal

calf (KAV) - a baby whale

extinction (ex TINK shun) - the end of a species

hemisphere (HEM i sfeer) - one half of the world

International Whaling Commission - an organization set up
  to control whaling

lagoon (la GOON) - a shallow bay

migrate (MI grayt) - to move from one place to another, usually at
  the same time each year

whalers (WHAYL ers) - people who hunt whales

World Wildlife Fund - an organization that helps save rare plants
  and animals

INDEX